**Lateral Leading**

*Stefan Kühl* is professor of sociology at the University of Bielefeld in Germany and works as a consultant for Metaplan, a consulting firm based in Princeton, Hamburg, Shanghai, Singapore, Versailles and Zurich. He studied sociology and history at the University of Bielefeld (Germany), Johns Hopkins University in Baltimore (USA), Université Paris-X-Nanterre (France) and the University of Oxford (UK).

## Other Books by Stefan Kühl

*Organizations: A Systems Approach*
(Routledge 2013)
*Ordinary Organizations: Why Normal Men Carried Out the Holocaust*
(Polity Press 2016)
*When the Monkeys Run the Zoo: The Pitfalls of Flat Hierarchies*
(forthcoming)
*Sisyphus in Management: The Futile Search for the Optimal Organizational Structure*
(forthcoming)
*The Rainmaker Effect: Contradictions of the Learning Organization*
(forthcoming)


To contact us:
Metaplan
101 Wall Street
Princeton, NJ 08540
USA
Phone: +1 609-688-9171
stefankuehl@metaplan.com
www.metaplan.com

# Stefan Kühl

# Lateral Leading

A Very Brief Introduction to Power, Understanding and Trust

Organizational Dialogue Press
Princeton, Hamburg, Shanghai, Singapore, Versailles, Zurich

ISBN (Print) 978-0-9991479-6-2
ISBN (EPUB) 978-0-9991479-7-9

Copyright © 2017 by Stefan Kühl

All rights reserved. No part of this publication may be reproduced or transmitted in any form or by any means, without permission in writing from the author.

Translated by: Lee Holt
Cover Design: Guido Klütsch
Typesetting: Thomas Auer
Project Management: Tabea Koepp
www.organizationaldialoguepress.com

# Contents

**Preface—Leading Beyond Hierarchical Control**.....................7

## 1.
**Lateral Leading—Introduction**..............................................13
   1.1 Applying the Concept.............................................................15
   1.2 On the Popularity of Lateral Leading....................................16

## 2.
**Power, Understanding and Trust—**
**The Three Pillars of Lateral Leading**.............................22
   2.1 Understanding—Overcoming Rigid Thought Structures .............23
   2.2 Power—The Control of Zones of Uncertainty...................26
   2.3 Trust—The Benefits and Dangers of Extending Trust....................29

## 3.
**The Interplay of the Three Mechanisms of Influence** ......33
   3.1 The Simultaneous Mode of Operation of Power,
       Understanding and Trust .........................................................34
   3.2 The Equal Ranking of the Three Mechanisms—
       Why You Cannot Prioritize Understanding, Power or Trust........37
   3.3 The Interplay of Power, Trust and Understanding............................39
   3.4 Mutual Replaceability—How Understanding,
       Power and Trust Can Replace One Another.......................................41

## 4.
## Connection to the Formal Structure of Organizations ........................................................................... 42
   4.1 The Genesis of Understanding, Power and Trust from an Organization's Structures ........................................................... 44
   4.2 The Influence of Understanding, Power and Trust in the Shadows of Formal Structure ...................................................... 46
   4.3 Understanding, Power and Trust— Limitations Caused by Integration in Organizations ...................... 49

## 5.
## How Do You Lead Laterally Through Processes of Change? Applying the Concept ................................................. 51
   5.1 The Initial Situation: The Logic of Innovation and Routines in Organizations ............... 54
   5.2 The Discussion Phase: The Potential of Lateral Cooperative Relationships ......................... 56
   5.3 The Creation of Change Processes: The Benefits of Contingency .................................................................. 59

## 6.
## Outlook—Additional "Search Fields" for Further Developing the Concept of Lateral Leading ........................... 62

## Bibliography ........................................................................................ 66

# Preface—Leading Beyond Hierarchical Control

It would be naive to describe hierarchy as an "outdated model" or to go so far as to assume that hierarchies should be "torn down, taken apart, and chopped up." The concepts of the learning organization and knowledge management, as well as deliberations about the decentralization of organization, have not dealt a mortal blow to hierarchies. There are good reasons to assume that as long as there are organizations, there will also be hierarchies. It seems that no other organizational mechanism is as well suited as hierarchy when it comes to making quick decisions, preventing constant power struggles, and pacifying conflicts at lower levels.

With increasing frequency, however, managers have the impression that hierarchical control in decision-making processes only works to a limited degree, and it appears that there are reasons for this. In the cooperative arrangements in a value-creation chain, there are often only limited ways to call for managerial intervention in conflict situations. This is because the more hierarchies are flattened out, the less available the hierarch becomes for the issuance of a "command" to solve coordination problems among subordinates. In collective bodies—for instance, works councils or the management boards of corporations—or in project groups with members from different departments, hierarchical coordination frequently has to be avoided, more or less. The "leader"—if there is even one at all—typically only holds a coordinating function and cannot solve conflicts by referring to a specific hierarchical position. The limits of hierarchical coordination become particularly clear in cooperation between various organizations. Employees of such organizations are often forced to bring up an issue without being sure that the details of their cooperative arrangement are clarified by contracts, or that their managers are even ready to clear up every small problem on the margins of a conference or—to invoke a cliché—on the golf course.

The concept of *lateral leading* tackles this problem and develops an approach to leadership that goes beyond hierarchy. The term itself may be irritating at first glance, because how can someone *lead* if they don't have any authority? The notion of lateral leading is an intentional oxymoron—a combination of two contradictory terms into one phrase—that seeks to make it clear that this concept is about bringing two dissonant demands into harmony. Just as the word "bittersweet" denotes that a dish can activate two opposed sets of taste buds, the special thing about the concept of lateral leading is the ability to lead without hierarchical authority.

Lateral leading is based on three central mechanisms of influence: understanding, power, and trust. *Understanding* means comprehending the structure of your counterpart's thinking in a way that creates new possibilities for action. *Trust* is built up if one side takes the risk of extending itself and the other side does not take short-term advantage of the situation, thereby showing itself worthy of trust. *Power* plays an important role in lateral leading, not in the form of hierarchical command structures, but rather on the basis of other sources of power, such as wielding control over internal, and often informal, communication, tapping into expert knowledge, or using contacts in the organization's environment.

This book briefly presents the idea of lateral leading, reviews experiences with it up to the present time, and advances the concept with a few central aspects. The challenge here is to avoid the classic schism of management science. One school of management science, shaped by classical business studies, focuses strongly on the formal structure of organizations, yet in the process neglects informal mechanisms of control. The other school of thought, shaped by human relations concerns and an interest in the question of "leadership by the powerless," has not adequately sought to find a connection to the formal structures of organization. Even if lateral leading seems at first glance to bear similarities with this school of management science, oriented as it is towards informal elements, it can only develop its full explanatory power if we incorporate considerations of the formal structure of organizations.

The first chapter traces the development of lateral leading as a concept. We will present various fields of application and assess the reasons for its popularity. The second chapter presents the three central mechanisms of influence in lateral leading—power, trust, and understanding—and their modes of function. The third chapter then shows how these three mechanisms of influence are connected. I believe that the core of the concept of lateral leading lies in the occasionally contentious interplay of these three mechanisms. The possibilities of lateral leading, however, have not even begun to be exhausted. The fourth chapter focuses on the embedding of processes of understanding, measures for establishing trust, and power games into the formal structures of organizations. Lateral leading is a concept that, for starters, opens up opportunities for action without having to fundamentally change the formal structures of a company, an administration, or an association. But everything that can be achieved with lateral leading is related to an organization's formal structures. The fifth chapter addresses the use of the concept in change processes, for example in the development of strategies or the reformation of organizational structures. The summary in the sixth chapter provides a brief overview of further ways in which the concept can be developed.

I wrote this book primarily for practitioners in companies, administrations, hospitals, universities, schools, armies, police forces, political parties, and associations. My presentation of our approach relies on several years of experience in working on change processes with companies, ministries, administrations, universities, hospitals, and non-profit organizations.

Even if the book is written out of practical experience and is meant for practical applications, I want the ideas described here to be coordinated with the modern approaches of organizational theory. Surely we cannot ignore the fundamentally different ways of thinking and commercial motives of organization theory on one hand and organizational practice on the other. The gap between organizational science and organizational practice cannot be fully closed (for management studies, see Kieser/Leiner 2009).

However, it is my ambition to present this approach, which has proven itself in practical applications, in such a way that it does not meet with the compassionate laughter of organizational scholars amused by its ostensibly truncated understanding of organizations (see for example March 2015, 153). Here and there, I have even tried—for example in the presentation of the connections between power, trust, and understanding, as well as the discussion of the relationship between formal and informal structure—to go beyond the current state of research, so that organizational scholars may find some stimulation in the book.

This slim volume is one of a series in which we introduce the essentials of major management topics, based on modern organizational theory. The *Management Compact* series includes books on the topics of *Designing Organizations, Influencing Organizational Culture, Developing Mission Statements, Managing Projects*, and *Exploring Markets*, along with *Lateral Leading* of course. These books can be read individually whenever a practitioner is confronted with a specific problem in an organization. The books are aligned in such a way, however, that they provide a coherent, balanced view of how organizations functions and how they can be influenced. Because we crafted the idea for these books at the same time, attentive readers will notice related trains of thought and similar formulations in all of the volumes in this series. These overlaps were created intentionally to emphasize the unity of the ideas behind the series and to highlight the connections between the volumes.

We do not believe in "simplifying" texts for managers and consultants by crowding our texts with bullet points, executive summaries, visual presentations of how the text flows, or exercises. In most cases, such methods infantilize readers because they suggest that they are not able to draw the central thoughts out of a book without these aids. That is why in this book, and in all of the other Management Compact volumes, we are very sparing with the use of visual aids. Along with a very limited number of graphics, there is only one element that makes reading easier: in small boxes, we introduce examples that give specific instances of our ideas, and we also mark more extensive connections to organizational theory. Readers who are short on time or are not interested in these aspects can skip over the text boxes without losing the thread.

You can read more about the theoretical foundations of organizations in my book, "Organizations: A Systems Approach" (Kühl 2013). I can recommend my trilogy to whoever is interested in locating the ideas in the Management Compact series within current discussions about management: "When the Monkeys Run the Zoo: The Pitfalls of Flat Hierarchies" (Kühl 2017), "Sisyphus in Management: The Futile Search for the Optimal Organizational Structure" (Kühl 2018a, forthcoming), and "The Rainmaker Effect: Contradictions of the Learning Organization" (Kühl 2018b, forthcoming).

This book was developed in the Metaplan training program, "Management and Consulting in Discourse." We would like to thank participants in the various courses for their input; they always critically assessed the approaches presented here and brought their practical experiences to the table. We are also grateful to those organizational scholars who have criticized and commented upon Metaplan's practices in recent decades.

# 1.
# Lateral Leading—Introduction

Members of an organization follow with great interest the subtle tactics, minor practices, and more or less skillful maneuvers that are executed and deployed in the shadows of hierarchy. These include for example the little tricks that simplify interactions in organizations and that can be used to get something done, even without authorization. We need think only of the tactfulness with which equally ranked colleagues interact, the banter and jokes in cooperative relationships, the exaggerated respect shown to influential people, the small voluntary efforts with which people seek to produce pleasure, or the gratitude that people express, even if this is not at all necessary within the formal organization (for more on these topics, Luhmann 1964, 331 remains unrivalled.).

We can view these tactics, practices and maneuvers as a more fluid, less disrupted arrangement of interactions in organizations. If we look at the innumerable management seminars on efficiently leading meetings, intercultural communication, quick-witted argumentation, strategic mediation, successfully motivating employees, emotional leadership, or diplomatic conflict management, then we recognize that all of these seminars focus on the same principal subject: strategic behavior in everyday interactions. They concentrate on such questions as how to control dynamics in meetings, what characterizes conflicts in interactions and how these contributing factors can be reduced, how to use one's own personality for persuasion in meetings, or how we can recognize and stimulate the intrinsic motivation of others in our everyday dealings.

Power, trust and understanding are the mechanisms of influence frequently concealed behind these interactions. Tactfulness, politeness and friendliness may be expected in interactions and practiced in leadership training sessions, yet they also significantly influence power, trust and understanding processes in organizations. Joking and teasing can certainly relax the mood of interactions, yet it also frequently has another important function if existing power, trust and understanding relationships are to be maintained or changed. Help and gratitude play a role in many interactions, even if there is no reason for such things in the context of a formal organizational structure; the operating principles are often only seen in processes of power, trust and understanding.

We use the term lateral leading as a handy term for describing the mechanisms of power, trust and understanding in the shadows of hierarchy. Certainly, power, trust and understanding play an important role both in lateral and hierarchical cooperative relationships. In the final analysis, whenever instructions are not followed by subordinates in a hierarchy, there must be other options for the exercise of power aside from threatening sanctions. The art of hierarchical leadership, as we know, can cover up informalities, or even illegalities, in an organization, because it creates a relationship of trust between the company's leadership and its subordinates. In lateral leading, these mechanisms of influence assume heightened importance because there is very limited recourse to the organization's hierarchy.

## 1.1 Applying the Concept

I assert that lateral leading is being used already in companies, administrations, hospitals, non-governmental organizations, political parties, and associations, even if most of the people involved don't have the word "laterality" in their vocabulary. Meetings, emails, or letters to colleagues are often at the same time processes of establishing understanding—attempts to convince others of your own position, and sometimes (even if rarely) attempts to understand others. The same is the case for trust. Almost every decision, many actions, and sometimes even a mere statement at a conference builds up a relationship of trust or mistrust among colleagues. The many minor strategies in cooperative relationships also serve to hint to colleagues at sources of power, to defend one's own power positions, or even to expand one's own power resources.

The concept of lateral leading makes it possible to study these processes of trust, understanding and power, which play out every day in organizations, and thereby, within limits, to change them. The idea of lateral leading helps to systematically analyze the understanding, power and trust resources of individual cooperation partners, as well as existing structures of understanding, power and trust.

The concept of lateral leading has been operationalized at several levels. The classical application of the concept is in the *training* of skilled staff and managers who have to manage cooperative relationships in more complex contexts without having hierarchical authority to issue directives. The concept of lateral leading has also proven itself in one-on-one *coaching*, in groups of people from different organizations, or in teams that always work together.

Problems are analyzed in the course of several sessions of people-oriented consulting, and appropriate analytical instruments are developed. In coaching in particular, there is a tendency to personify problems. Based on a systematic reconnection of all analytical and intervention instruments to organizational structures, the concept of lateral leading is better suited than other approaches for identifying the organizational starting point for suitable solutions. Developments in recent years have increasingly gone in the direction of custom-tailoring the concept for application in *leadership in change processes*. These efforts have focused primarily on mapping out the specifics of power, trust and understanding in the design of organizational structures, the development of strategies, or the development of major themes, thereby providing managers and consultants with a more exact approach.

## 1.2 On the Popularity of Lateral Leading

In the 1950s, the idea emerged that leadership is not just a top-down phenomenon; it could also come from the side, or even from the bottom to the top, in the form of employees monitoring supervisors. There have been repeated attempts, under terms such as "lateral relationships," "lateral cooperation," "lateral cooperation styles," "lateral management," or "lateral leadership" (see for example Strauss 1962; Yukl/Falbe 1990; Fisher/Sharpe 1998), to develop practical approaches for leadership without the authority to issue directives. But in the last few years in particular, lateral leadership has become quite popular, not just in the management press, but also because of its implementation in a broad array of fields and through the development of different seminar concepts. How can we explain this?

First, members of organizations appear to be increasingly searching for ways to influence others, and they don't want to have to refer to hierarchy to wield this influence. Even if there was a trend toward flattening hierarchies—and thereby a search for alternative mechanisms of control—as early as the 1920s, many managers today often find themselves again and again in situations in which they have to make decisions without having the appropriate hierarchical authorization to do so. Lateral leading represents an alternative to many leadership techniques because it is not situated primarily at the level of personal leadership competence; instead, it is integrated systematically within an organization and its structures. In this regard, lateral leading is part of a trend toward "post-heroic management" (Handy 1989), in which the focus has shifted from the charismatic powers of a leader to an approach, practiced by the organization's members, that is systematically incorporated into an organizational analysis.

Second, external consultants are even more dependent than an organization's members when it comes to using mechanisms of influence outside of the hierarchical structure of authorization. Fundamental consulting skills therefore include the formation of processes of communication and understanding, knowledge of power games, and the development of trust processes. The concept of lateral leading makes it possible to systematically combine these starting points, which already exist in the consultant's toolkit of expertise. In this respect, the concept may be a welcome rationalization for consultants to continue doing what they already do; on the other hand, it enables them to construct a framework in which power, trust and understanding can be systematically related to one another.

Third, recent decades of organizational research have yielded a number of interesting explanatory approaches to how understanding is reached in organizations, how power games develop, or how trust and distrust emerge. We need only point to debates in systems theory, rational choice theory, and behavioral decision theory, which is currently dominating organizational science. These theories, which are not always easily accessible through scholarly texts, can be interesting to practitioners for precisely this reason, because they sow fundamental doubts (which have also been broadly accepted in scholarship) about instrumental-rational organizational concepts from classical business studies, as well as some of the approaches to organizational development that rest on authority-free discourses. The concept of lateral leading represents an opportunity to communicate modern approaches in organizational research and to transfer considerations from organizational research—at least partially—into instruments of analysis and intervention.

## THEORY

### The Paradigm Shift in the Concept of Lateral Leading

Organizational researchers noted very early on that both hierarchical and laterally oriented leadership processes play a central role in companies, administrations, hospitals and NGOs.

Beginning in the 1960s, the term "lateral organizational relationships" emerged as a way to describe these relationships that existed outside of hierarchies (see Walton 1966).

A number of case studies at the time showed that very different types of organizations are shaped by lateral cooperative relationships. At one U.S. textile company, researchers were able to prove that a majority of coordination within the firm took place at the lateral level (see also Simpson 1959). A study of the coordination between two departments within one social aid institution demonstrated that coordination typically ran without intervention from the hierarchy, despite formal instructions to the contrary (see Blau/Scott 1962, 159). Even armies—the prototypes of hierarchically structured organizations—were shown to rely frequently on lateral mechanisms of coordination to face more complex challenges (see Janowitz 1959).

The early theoretical discussion about lateral cooperative relationships was shaped by the contingency approach then dominant in organizational theory. This approach focused on the search for the right fit between environmental conditions and organizational structure. The more diverse an organization's environment is, and the faster markets, knowledge and political conditions change, then the stronger the efforts an organization has to make to decentralize, the weaker the hierarchical intervention options become, and the more strongly lateral cooperative relationships develop (see Burns/Stalker 1961 and Lawrence/Lorsch 1967, which are characteristic for this approach).

The approach proffered by contingency theory, however, is limited because it only can make statements (and sometimes recommendations) about the number and intensity of lateral cooperative relationships. Despite extensive efforts, this approach never got farther than the statement, "The more complex the environment, the more laterality in the organization." Apparently there was a lack of insight into how lateral cooperative relationships form and which mechanisms operate within them, which means that there was an absolute dearth of ideas about how to change them.

Attempts to make lateral leadership tangible for organizational practice often relied primarily on individual recommendations for improved negotiation management. The motto was: "Improve your capabilities for inserting yourself into the group as a lateral leader by further developing your personal capabilities." Specific recommendations for action came in the form of maxims such as, "involve your colleagues in plans for change," "remain receptive," "ask your colleagues to share their thoughts," "ask real questions," or "offer your thoughts" (see Fisher/Sharpe 1998, 23).

The paradigm shift in the concept of lateral leading—what makes it different from communications seminars, presentation trainings, and team workshops—is the embedding of the concept more deeply into an organization's processes. The people involved in lateral leading are viewed as role bearers in an organization. Their interests and thought structures are assumed to be the expression of their organizational position, and the concept of lateral leading must therefore attach consistently to the organizational involvement of the "lateral leaders." The effects that can be generated by the three coordination mechanisms of "understanding," "power" and "trust" therefore depend not only on the personality of the actors involved, but also on the organizational structures under analysis.

The focus on the three influencing mechanisms of "understanding," "power" and "trust" connects to considerations from control theory, which strives to develop various mechanisms that increase the probability that something will happen.

# 2.
# Power, Understanding and Trust— The Three Pillars of Lateral Leadership

The likelihood is slim that our behavioral expectations of another will meet with that person's acceptance. Certainly another person sometimes behaves out of his own interest in a way that we can expect, and then we could attribute that behavior to our own expectations; but typically we have to provide social "assistance" so that a counterpart will behave in line with our own expectations.

In organizational science, the means with which one can assert behavioral expectations against others is described as *mechanisms of influence* (for a very quick introduction to the term "influence," see Luhmann 1979). In the terminology of systems theory, the use of mechanisms of influence increases the probability that others will accept the behavioral expectations communicated.

The necessity of using mechanisms of influence arises through the simple fact that the participants in a group, a family, an organization, a protest organization, or even a spontaneous face-to-face interaction at a conference, rock concert, or while waiting in a line, are dependent on one another and therefore have a "positive attitude" when it comes to "trying to reach and receive" others (Luhmann 2002, 40). The creation of understanding, the use of power, and the building of trust are the central mechanisms here (for alternative proposals, see Luhmann 1979).

## 2.1 Understanding—Overcoming Rigid Thought Structures

There are always ossified patterns of thinking in organizations everywhere. Every actor is connected to a group whose expectations must be met. A group's thought structure is normally coherent and self-contained. People have developed joint attitudes about how they view reality and their place in it. Explanatory models also become dogmatic, meaning that they are no longer subject to questioning.

The typical thought structures for a group can arise from the standards, norms and attitudes of a professional community; one need only think of attorneys, physicians, or engineers. In organizations, such patterns of thinking arise from functional differentiation, as a result of the division of labor. Ways of thinking in sales, for example, are oriented towards the satisfaction of customer desires, while the production department's patterns of thought are focused on preventing changes to current and planned production.

EXAMPLE

### Example: Rigid Attitudes at Fashionable Wear

The following example shows how attitudes and opinions become rigid. In a textile factory that we'll call Fashionable Wear, there are three groups that want to talk about customer demand for brand-name products. The representatives of these groups are, first, the production manager; second, the designer and product manager; and third, the management with its controlling function. They have the following attitudes:

The production manager believes that large runs can only be produced with modern machines. The entire production program should be "run through" in one shot; there will be no conversions for special requests. The design has to be produced in a rational manner.

The designer and the product manager think that you can only command good prices with brand products. The brand-name clothing line must always be up-to-date, meaning fashionable, and its design can change at short notice. They believe that design quality is crucial for success.

Controlling and management think that the brand connects customers to the company. To be successful, the company needs modern machines and production methods, so that they can manufacture "mass with class."

These different ways of thinking make understanding difficult: the production manager dreams of a high-tech production line; for the designer and product manager, only creativity and fashion sense count; and management believes that creative design and high-tech production need not be mutually exclusive.

Whenever we talk about rigid ways of thinking, we don't mean that they are absolutely fixed and immobile. They are completely capable of change, just like interests, beliefs, standards, etc.—yet changing ways of thinking is extremely tedious and slow. The following questions can help identify rigid patterns of thinking in organizations: Which (basic) beliefs in one group disturb those of another group; which beliefs do not fit together? Which (self-serving) interests does one group attribute to the other, and which interests are disclosed openly? Which work routines obstruct the view? What thoughts are people afraid of in an organization? Which beliefs within a group are contradictory? When does a group act in a way that is at odds with its own beliefs?

The starting point is that people can come to an agreement within an organization through communication and understanding about how a specific task should be completed. Coordination through understanding requires a shared background of experience that forces everyone to take into account the diverging interests of other participants and to think about the effects of their own actions. This allows for a reduction of interpretive effort and of the risk of dissent to such a degree that communication can lead to a fiction of consensus.

The advantages associated with management through understanding are obvious: understanding, as a mechanism of coordination, mobilizes the views, experience and interests of several actors. People hope thereby to find the best possible solution for a specific task. Processes of understanding within companies reduce management's problems with motivation and monitoring. Employees select a specific way to deal with a problem because they have agreed on this approach with everyone else involved, not because they see themselves as forced to do so by orders or by market processes. The hope here is that measures of motivation and control can fall away.

## 2.2 Power—The Control of Zones of Uncertainty

Power is part of every relationship. Power is the mechanism people use to produce behavior in others that they would not have engaged in spontaneously. The exercise of power enables one actor to structure a (more or less long) process of exchange in such a way that this one actor can draw advantages from the situation (Friedberg 1993, 117). Power is a relationship of exchange that may be asymmetrical, yet is always mutual. A person or a group of people can only push through their own beliefs if another person or group is prepared to enter into a relationship with them. A departmental director can only issue instructions as long as the employees submit to these instructions. As soon as a person quits, for example, or changes positions within the firm, the exchange relationship is over, and with it the power relationship. If someone refused to work overtime hours, for example, this can put the departmental director in a predicament, which is why supervisors often have to offer "their" people compensation in such cases. Both sides therefore always draw advantages from a power relationship. Of course, this does not mean that the process of exchange has to be fair or just. It does suggest, however, that even the ostensibly powerless have an interest in maintaining a power relationship.

Power depends on the wielder's relevance for others and their own irreplaceability. A sales employee who has privileged access to an important customer has a dog in the hunt, and he can use that to his advantage. The more irreplaceable an IT expert is because of her detailed knowledge of an internal company program, the stronger her position against people who depend on this program.

Conflicts in power relationships tend to be the exception rather than the rule, yet there are conflict situations in which the special significance of power as a mechanism of influence becomes apparent. Power relationships are based on the fact that they are shared by the participants and more or less accepted. Although the threat always looms in the background that one could allow an opposing interest to escalate, a power relationship is typically characterized by both sides complying and holding their sanctions and threats at bay, only alluding to them carefully.

Power is based on the control of zones of uncertainty. According to Crozier and Friedberg (1980), the following zones of uncertainty are typical for organizations: (a) *hierarchies* draw their influence from their ability to issue formal organizational rules that can narrow or expand the field of action for subordinates; (b) *experts*, for example IT experts or marketing specialists, substantiate their influential position by means of their mastery of specialized knowledge that is relevant to the organization; (c) people who represent *relay stations* to the environment draw their power from their privileged access to customers, central suppliers, important cooperation partners, or influential state positions; (d) *gate keepers*, such as a secretary or personal assistant, base their influence upon the control they wield over important internal communication channels and information sources.

Hierarchy therefore rules over just one zone of uncertainty, which is why we should not equate hierarchy with power. Certainly, managers don't just make decisions about work processes or strategies; they also play a significant role in the hiring, firing and career development of their employees. They therefore control a central zone of uncertainty for their employees, at least as long as the latter do not have more attractive alternatives on the job market. At the same time, they can also hold control over other zones of uncertainty, such as contact to the environment or specialized knowledge, but not automatically, sort of ex officio. Subordinates often possess more specialized knowledge than their superiors. Due to the growing need for specialized knowledge, managers often cannot maintain an overview of all of the subjects within their domain and have to rely on their employees to be more expert and competent than they are. Contacts with customers, suppliers, cooperation partners or political institutions are no longer a monopoly held by the top of the organization. Particularly in larger companies, administrations and associations, it is necessary for organizational heads to delegate the maintenance of external contacts. Managers often do not have the opportunity to regulate all of the communications in their organizations. The fact that managers often complain about (ostensibly false) rumors shows that communication in companies takes a completely different course than managers would prefer.

Even if a process is managed via lateral leading, we still find situations in which the power mechanism of "hierarchy" only functions in a limited way (if at all). But even in situations in which clear hierarchical relations exist, the management effects of hierarchy remain limited because subordinates also control important zones of uncertainty. In hospitals, for example, the supposed "gods in white coats" do not have full decision-making power over processes, despite their formal authorizations. Nurses dominate zones of uncertainty that are important for doctors, and they can use these as an element of exchange. This means that doctors are dependent on nurses because the doctors themselves only spend brief amounts of time with the patients. Physicians have to rely on nurses taking over administrative, and sometimes curative, tasks. This can lead to the emergence of negotiating conditions in which nurses trade in their willingness to take on more responsibility for more say in how patients are treated. Even in prisons, the prisoners are not fully at the mercy of their guards. Although guards can report prisoner misconduct and call for punishment, this would convey the impression that they don't have a grip on their prisoners. To avoid this, relations of exchange arise in which the guards allow the prisoners a few violations of the rules as long as they continue to cooperate in general (see Mechanic 1962).

Despite all of this, power games are not dysfunctional for organizations. To the contrary: they contribute significantly to the overcoming of obstacles that would arise in terms of the impossibility of being able to make rational decisions. They are the grease that keeps the gears of the organization in motion.

## 2.3 Trust—The Benefits and Dangers of Extending Trust

Cooperation is risky. One person's actions depend on what others are doing. The same applies to the actions of these other parties if they want to connect with this one person's actions. Respective manners of action are not predictable with any certainty; they are contingent. Trust offers a way for cooperation to happen despite this contingency.

The problem is that, if you want to trust others, you enter into a risky situation that is very difficult to assess in advance. In contrast to the exercise of power—which includes the option of being able to make threats with negative sanctions in the event your expectations are not met—trust means exposing yourself more or less to the risk of being taken advantage of.

Unlike power relationships, trust relationships do not entail a quantification of goods of exchange, and the exchange process need not be completed immediately. Trust relationships are relationships of exchange "without equivalent certainty" (Luhmann 1979). Real estate investors, for example, are increasingly departing from the practice of squeezing every last drop out of general contractors during negotiations, because it became clear that general contractors would have their revenge during the finishing phase. Instead, real estate investors are trying to establish a process in which they grant general contractors trust in advance and assume that, in return, they will not exploit their strong position later.

Trust stabilizes trusting behavior as an output and flows into further activity has a foundation of trust. A delayed social exchange takes place. One side invests trust in the other, expecting that they will prove that they are worthy of this trust and can also bring trust to the table. For example, those employees with whom managers already have experience, and have deemed trustworthy, are granted such trust (see Mayer et al. 1995, 712; Schoorman et al. 2007, 344).

The more often advance trust from one side is honored by the other side, the more likely it is that a long-term relationship of trust will develop. This leads to a self-reinforcing mechanism that stabilizes to the degree at which expectations are met by the counterparty.

The central advantage of trust as a mechanism of influence is that trust is a strategy with a very broad scope of action. If there is trust, then you do not need to expect immediate rewards for a service. There is no need to figure out who is stronger, to nail everything down with meticulously precise contracts. Wherever there is trust, according to a somewhat esoteric-sounding assumption in systems theory, there is an increased contingency of experience and action (see Luhmann 1979).

The problem, however, is that the smallest sign of a breach of trust can be enough to end the relationship. The cost-cutting policy that an automobile corporation's managing director can dictate from above to suppliers can lead to the destruction of a trusting relationship between a company and its suppliers, built up over a long time, because the suppliers could perceive a cost-cutting policy as the "termination" of trusting cooperation, leading them to react with less goodwill when it comes to the non-contractual elements of the relationship.

We should not overlook the fact that distrust—despite all of the word's negative connotations—is also a way to come to a cooperative agreement. The advantage of a strategy based on distrust is that the risk for the cooperating parties is very low. People only enter into cooperative arrangements if they are prepared for all eventualities, for example through contractual assurances or shoring up their own power basis. An automobile company's strategy of squeezing suppliers and getting as much as possible out of them through an adhesion contract is one strategy for getting things done. This may even turn out to be more cost-effective for the company than previously practiced forms of cooperation. But the organization pays for the shift from a trust to distrust strategy with decreased flexibility in the relationship.

The interesting part, however, is that—as mentioned earlier—often a minor incident is enough to flip a relationship of trust into one of distrust. Distrust, in contrast, cannot be converted back as quickly to trust; such a shift can only take place gradually.

# 3.
# The Interplay of the Three Mechanisms of Influence

When I say that three mechanisms of influence are at work in lateral leading—understanding, power and trust—I am going quite far out on a limb. This concept's focus on understanding, power and trust suggests that precisely these three mechanisms are applied, and that, accordingly, the art of lateral leading lies in the application of precisely these three mechanisms.

At first glance, stringing together the terms understanding, power and trust reminds us of the Chinese encyclopedia described by the Argentine writer Jorge Luis Borges (1999, 299). This list—which purports to be an historical document, yet was actually made up by Borges—groups animals in China as follows: a) those that belong to the emperor; b) embalmed ones; c) those that are trained; d) suckling pigs; e) sirens; f) mythical creatures; g) stray dogs; h) those that are included in this classification; i) those that tremble as if they were mad; j) innumerable ones; k) those drawn with a very fine camel hair brush; l) et cetera; m) those that have just broken the flower vase; n) those that, at a distance, resemble flies.

Isn't the concatenation of understanding, power and trust a similar list—a nearly random string of ideas and concepts? What do understanding, power and trust in organizations have in common? Why have we chosen these three mechanisms and not other ones? How do these three mechanisms fit together? What do we gain by choosing precisely these three mechanisms?

To justify working with these three mechanisms, we have to show that understanding, trust and power can be delineated from one another, that no one of these three mechanisms dominate the other two, and that—at least partially—they can substitute for each other.

## 3.1 The Simultaneous Mode of Operation of Power, Understanding and Trust

A joke much loved by organizational researchers can illustrate how mechanisms of power, trust and understanding work in cooperations: "During the Stalin era in the Soviet Union, an orchestra conductor was on the train, heading to his next performance, and was looking at the sheet music for the piece that he was going to conduct that evening. Two KGB officers watched him, and because they thought that the sheet music had to be a secret code, they arrested the man as a spy. He protested and explained that the music was only a violin concerto by Tchaikovsky, but nothing helped. On the second day of his imprisonment, his interrogator came in, sure of victory, and said: "You had better tell us everything. We also caught your friend Tchaikovsky, and he's already confessed to everything."

Both of the KGB prisoners—the conductor and Tchaikovsky—find themselves caught in the prisoner's dilemma, which was first elaborated by Albert Tucker. Two defendants are accused of committing a crime together. They have to decide whether or not to confess, without knowing what the other person has decided to do. If only one prisoner—the conductor or Tchaikovsky—confessed, then he would be granted leniency and let go. The other would end up in prison for ten years. If both confess, then each receives a five-year sentence. If no one confesses, they would be sentenced to one year for using a secret code.

| B (Tchaikovsky) <br> A (Conductor) | Cooperation with A (Conductor) (Denial) | Non-cooperation with A (Conductor) (Confess) |
|---|---|---|
| Cooperation with B (Tchaikovsky) (Denial) | -1,-1 | -10,-0 |
| Non-cooperation with B (Tchaikovsky) (Confess) | - 0, -10 | -5,-5 |

**Table:** The Prisoner's Dilemma

At first glance, it seems the best decision is for both to confess. The conductor may think to himself, if Tchaikovsky also confesses, then I can reduce my possible sentence from ten to five years; if he refuses to say anything, then I can even get leniency by turning state's witness. Confessing seems to be a sensible strategy for Tchaikovsky, although it would be best for the both of them to remain silent, meaning that they would be cooperating (see Rapoport/Chammah 1965 for the first early, thorough description of the prisoner's dilemma).

The prisoner's dilemma, in whatever form, is interesting for our purposes because it shows how the three coordination mechanisms of understanding, power and trust (could) work in this situation. If the two prisoners come to an agreement—for example, by being interrogated together—then it is easy for both of them to adopt a cooperative strategy of denial. If there is a deep trust between the two prisoners, built up over several years, then both can assume that the other will keep quiet. Even if one person has a great deal of power over the other, it is still possible for the two prisoners to come to a cooperative strategy. It is well known that the Italian mafia has managed to ensure that people held in custody remain quiet, despite the isolation of the prisoners and the offer to turn state's evidence, by threatening their families. The prisoner's dilemma only becomes a dilemma at all because all three of the possible coordination mechanisms available to the two prisoners—understanding, power and trust—can be disabled by external forces, and the effect of one of these mechanisms would suffice to solve the dilemma.

In reality, all three mechanisms almost always play a role in cooperation. Processes of understanding, power and trust always run simultaneously in the organization (and not just there). Often it isn't possible to recognize in a discussion what is actually happening: is the project manager trying out a new trick in a power game? Is he attempting to manufacture agreement about specific positions? Or is he seeking a "trust-building measure"?

## 3.2 The Equal Ranking of the Three Mechanisms— Why You Cannot Prioritize Understanding, Power or Trust

In management literature and in scholarly research on organizations, there are always repeated attempts to assign greater significance to one of the three mechanisms of influence. Depending on taste, experience or a catalog of values, either understanding, power or trust is declared as the central mechanism of management in an organization. This becomes particularly clear in openly propagated management concepts.

With ideas such as "discursive organizations," "democratic companies," or "consensual management," for example, *understanding* is raised up to a central form of management in and between organizations. The idea here is that people can come to an agreement within an organization through communication and understanding about how a specific task should be completed. The advantages associated with management through understanding are obvious: it mobilizes the views, experience and interests of several actors. People hope to use understanding to find the best solution for a specific task. Processes of understanding and negotiation reduce management's problems with motivation and monitoring. Employees select a specific way to deal with a problem because they have agreed on this approach with everyone else involved, not because they see themselves as forced to do so by orders or market processes. The hope here is that measures of motivation and control can fall away.

Even the widespread extreme stylization of *trust* as a central mechanism of control illuminates the romanticized view of many managers, in which the elimination of a "distrust organization" leads to the fulfillment of their dreams. "Trust leads," "trust conquers," or "success through trust" are key catchwords in the current management discussion. The greater the perceived uncertainties in organizations, the more frequently we see attempts to coordinate collaboration between various entities via trust-building measures. We can interpret the broad propagation of the "trust organization," and thereby an organizational culture based on trust, as an index of the "moralization of commercial social contexts."

Yet *power* is also a frequently used tool in management concepts. Both the biographies of "great corporate leaders" and guidebooks such as "Machiavelli for Managers" understand organizations as a lion's den in which the members fight against each other with all of the means at their disposal. Cooperation within and between organizations then takes on the appearance of major power struggles. Even in the scholarly literature, there is the idea of declaring "micro-politics"—the power games that go on every day—as a central mechanism in organizations.

Discourse about management is oriented towards the current spirit of the times, so it makes sense for management gurus to push one mechanism at some times, another at other times. If an idea of "daring democracy" permeates the general social level, then we can see in the management literature how consultants and managers jump on the bandwagon of concepts meant to produce agreement. If the situation gets worse in companies, administration or political parties, then the concepts that are currently in vogue prescribe the propagation of the game while "taking the gloves off" and presenting the exercise of power as a central secret to power. A few years later, interactions based on trust are promoted as a recipe for success, sometimes by the same management gurus.

To avoid misunderstanding, we should point out that those who advance understanding, those who are exponents of power, and agitators for trust all hit the mark—in the final analysis, each of these three mechanisms play an important role in coordination within and between organizations. In reality, we see that one of these mechanisms is often favored, and the privileged mechanism changes frequently. Sometimes, you can recognize very quickly that cooperation is based on a trusting relationship that has grown up over a long period of time; sometimes you realize that cooperation advances because all of the stakeholders can reach agreements; and sometimes, you see that more or less skillful power games dominate a cooperative relationship. There is no meta-mechanism, though—outside of the dreams of management gurus—that is more predominant than the others.

It is therefore of secondary importance whether we analyze a cooperative relationship through the lens of power, trust or understanding, whether a training session focuses on one of the mechanisms, or which of these three mechanisms is selected as a point of departure for an upcoming process of change.

## 3.3 The Interplay of Power, Trust and Understanding

In the context of everyday cooperation in organizations, the lack of clarity about which form of coordination—understanding, building trust or power games—is going on at the moment is actually helpful. This creates a larger field of possible actions because what is said and what is done can be interpreted in different ways. In order to systematize the processes of lateral leading, however, it is important to recognize how understanding, power and trust are related to one another.

Power, trust and understanding frequently intermesh in such a way that they mutually support each other. If there is trust, then it is often easier to reach agreement and understanding. People initially assume that the other person doesn't want to pull them over a barrel and that it is up to them to exchange differing appraisals. If one person has too much power in a relationship, he can force the other to join up with his own ideas—for example, by "requesting" a meeting with others. Whether they are open to an intensive process of building understanding is of course another issue. If people are in the middle of a process of building understanding and gain some insight into the pressures faced by others, then it may be easier to convert a relationship of distrust into one of trust.

Processes of understanding, power and trust, however, can also work against each other. Shaking up existing structures of thought brings to light information that others can use in power games. If one person signals in a blatantly obvious way that he controls a zone of uncertainty that is central for the others, this can make building up relationships of trust difficult. If you want to establish relationships of trust, it is not a good idea to force through your own interests with power.

There is no proper mixture of trust, power and understanding for all forms of cooperation. In the course of analyzing these processes, however, perhaps we can show which of these mechanisms is better suited to producing the desired effect in specific cooperative relationships. The trick lies precisely in the setting of priorities in certain situations.

## 3.4 Mutual Replaceability—How Understanding, Power and Trust Can Replace One Another

A particularly interesting feature in the process of lateral leading is the fact that processes of understanding, power and trust can replace one another, at least partially. If distrust creeps into a cooperative relationship, it may be necessary to develop new power games to get things moving forward. If there is trust, then you do not need to understand the thought structures of others. You can move forward without knowing precisely what is driving your counterpart.

Specifically, this means that the concept of lateral leading offers the option of watching out for what are called functional equivalents. You can look for processes that could deliver results similar to those of the process that doesn't seem to work at the moment. If you are dealing with an entrenched power game, a cooperation partner can attempt, by leading a discussion, to open up closed structures of thought, thereby creating understanding rather than engaging in power struggles. This can lead either to an increase in the rationality of a decision, or to the creation of new rules of the game, as a compromise. If a cooperation partner recognizes that he cannot get any further through processes of understanding because local rationalities differ too strongly, then he can open up other power games by bringing in new actors, through exchange platforms, or by creating new rules. This may lead to one side being able to assert itself.

# 4.
# Connection to the Formal Structure of Organizations

Understanding, power and trust play a role in every social relationship. If we examine families for instance, we see how (blind) trust develops between the spouses, how they struggle to find agreement on how to raise their children, or how subtle power games emerge so that one partner can bring the other to do what is expected of him or her. In groups—whether they be circles of friends, cliques of adolescents, street gangs, "independent" leftist political groups, or small terrorist cells—we can see how trust (or distrust) develops, how they wrestle with understanding, and how power games arise. Even for small, regular meetings, such as those among grocers, these mechanisms are in play to some extent: a loyal customer may write a letter in an attempt to understand why a product has become so much more expensive, or the customer may threaten (often in unspoken ways) to switch to the newly opened grocer around the corner.

What is special about the ways in which understanding, power and trust operate in organizations? What are the consequences if lateral leading takes place in (or between) organizations?

In an imaginary perfect organization, you wouldn't have to think at all about power, understanding and trust. In the perfect organization—if we allow ourselves to entertain this mental game—the people who have authority over specific questions would be governed on one hand by the hierarchy and on the other by the formation of departments. When responsibilities are clearly established, there is no room for power games. In the perfect organization, everyone would know about everything that affects their position, and everyone would be very well informed. Everyone would understand everyone else's logic and ways of thinking. This would render understanding unnecessary. Furthermore, behavior in the perfect organization would be so predictable thanks to "clear structures" that people could rely on one another. There would be no loopholes that would have to be sealed up by trust between people.

Managers of companies, administrations, hospitals and NGOs strive toward this ideal world, by constantly perfecting their policies, the constant redefinition of responsibilities, or adjusting the organizational structure, which is often supported by consultants. The ideal situation reminds us of Charlie Chaplin in the film "Modern Times," in which he presents a caricature of the organization as a clockwork in which all of the parts intermesh perfectly.

It may be possible to attain, at least for a period of time, the status of a "perfect organization" in the "value-generating core" of some companies, administrations or NGOs. The specific manufacturing processes in production, the processing of social aid applications, the distribution of food to the ill, or the dispatch of appeals for donations—all of this may be standardized to such a degree that there is no opportunity or necessity for power games, trust-building measures or processes of understanding. A fully standardized "value-generating core" can only arise, however, if departments such as production planning, warehousing or human resources absorb constant uncertainties from the environment (Thompson 1967, 21).

Wherever routines have to be discarded in organizations, where behavior cannot be prescribed or dictated, wherever people work together across their functions—that's where the mechanisms of understanding, trust and power are at work.

## 4.1 The Genesis of Understanding, Power and Trust from an Organization's Structures

It is often assumed that a company's business goals, an administration's policy provisions, or a political party platform also determine the goals of the corresponding organizational units. People believe that an intelligent structural design can enable an organization's uppermost goals to be cleanly broken down into sub-goals that are then taken on by a team, section or department. From this perspective, deviations by individual organizational units from the business goals, guidelines or programs are only conceivable as pathological behavior that has to be brought under control by the hierarchy.

Research on organizations conducted before the Second World War, however, had already made clear the limitations of this approach. Of course, the individual departments have to refer—at least rhetorically—to the organization's overall goals; their actions, however, are determined primarily by the specific requirements assigned to the departments. For the individual organizational unit, reaching their own targets is more important than hitting the overall target. The tasks assigned to the units determine their rationality—the criteria that define it, as well as the kinds of thoughts and actions that are viewed as reasonable. Each unit thereby develops very specific criteria for "professional excellence."

These highly specific criteria for "professional excellence" are internalized by members of the respective organizational unit. No member of the organization, according to Nobel Prize winner Herbert A. Simon (1976, ), would be able to work for several months or years in a certain position in an organization without profound changes in what he knows, believes, and hopes. One way to see how much an organizational position can shape its holder is to observe what happens—in terms of changes with regard to knowledge, attitudes and positions—when a person is moved to another position in the organization. A departmental director in a top staff position who always pushed for the company to have a uniform outward appearance then changes her attitude, suddenly and surprisingly, when transferred to a new job in operations.

"Local rationalities," in the final analysis, determine the attitudes held by organizational units, as well as the people working within them. The individual organizational units develop their own opinions about what their respective "reality" is and how they should understand their position in it. These views are then interwoven with interests to that effect about what the respective organizational unit wants to achieve or deflect. Thus the sales department develops a rationality that is oriented towards selling as many products as possible. The question of how much it costs to make these products is considered tangentially, if at all. The rationality of the production department, however, is primarily fixated on the optimal utilization of machines and human resources. The marketability of these "optimally manufactured products" is thought to be someone else's problem.

In brief: the often opposing views, interests and positions within organizations are significantly affected by the organization's structure. Structures, according to Niklas Luhmann (1969, 3), provide a "permanent pre-selection" of what is possible in a company, administration, hospital or non-profit organization. The leeway in lateral leading inheres to the application of more or less tactically skillful strategies of understanding, trust and power.

So how do these three mechanisms of influence relate to an organization's formal structure?

## 4.2 The Influence of Understanding, Power and Trust in the Shadows of Formal Structure

Organizations have the distinctive feature of being able to "formalize" the three mechanisms of influence: power, trust and understanding (see Luhmann 1964, 123). There are aspects of power that are secured by the organization. This includes not just the hierarchy but also the power that one is granted through the hierarchy; for example, the special deputy of the boss, an external person granted the authority to conduct negotiations, or the right of a few select people to cast a veto against certain decisions. Trust can also be formalized. Along with trust placed in people, there is also trust in organizations—the reliability that work contracts are valid; that salaries are paid and, if not, can be claimed in court; that a certain department will deliver information because the rules stipulate it (Luhmann 1964, 72). Furthermore, understanding in organizations can be arranged in a very limited framework, for example by setting up regular meetings to coordinate between two departments.

The mechanisms of influence that are important in the concept of lateral leading tend to manifest their effects in the shadows of formal structure. Although it is indeed the formal structure that enables cooperation partners to set up, consolidate and develop their sources of power—when it comes to power games, people tend however to resort to minor tactical moves to take care of their own interests. The situation is similar with regard to trust. It seems at first glance that personal trust is unnecessary. Employees go along with the boss (even if reluctantly) because that is what the organization stipulates, and the boss and the employees can rely on this up to a certain degree. You can count on your salary being paid and your work contract being honored, even if your mentor has just left the company. In the shadow of system trust, however, trust between people very much plays an important role in organizations. If the boss wants his employees to stay beyond their regular working hours, he needs the employees to trust that their goodwill will be honored at some point down the road. If you don't just want to remain in the organization in the security of a work contract, but want to pursue a career, networks based on trust between people will help. Processes of reaching agreement and understanding also seem to be superfluous in organizations. First, people can rely on things getting done because the organization demands it. Yet there are also processes running in the shadows of the formal structure in which people try to understand the other's position, and to make their own position comprehensible.

The "paradox of the organization chart" is that formal structures generate problems because they don't cover all of the demands of daily business and therefore cannot (or cannot be permitted to) prevent divergent informal behavior. Rules, which are supposed to reduce uncertainty in organizations, call for deviations from the rules every day, which brings new uncertainty into the organization. The stability created by rules, which serve as fixed points by which organizations can orient their decisions, are counteracted by the fact that deviations from these rules must always be taken into consideration. Organizational practice requires adaptable rules from which momentary deviations are possible without completely invalidating the rules.

The willingness to deviate from the rules "in the context of the organization" is always implicitly demanded from employees. However, this willingness cannot—and this is distinctive—be claimed through the hierarchy's formal sanction options. And it is precisely this discrepancy between officially prescribed obligations and the actual behavior expected that can become the source of power and influence for employees lower on the hierarchy: important resources arise that are traded on the exchanges within an organization. As David Mechanic (1962) pointed out in the 1960s, real options for ostensibly "powerless" employees arise through the possibility (and necessity) of independent control of work performance and the functional redefinition of tasks.

These processes of power, trust and understanding can also develop because they are not forced, prohibited or required by the organization's formal structure. "Real" understanding cannot be coerced in an organization. Power games cannot be legally prohibited. Trust between people cannot be mandated through the hierarchy. At the same time, however, an organization's formal structure plays a central role in ensuring that processes for negotiating power, trust and understanding in organizations do not become excessive.

## 4.3 Understanding, Power and Trust—Limitations Caused by Integration in Organizations

Organizations differ from other social structures, such as family and circles of friends, in that processes of power, trust and understanding are circumscribed by a formal structure. In contrast to organizations, there are only a few, comparatively late-acting social braking mechanisms in families, particularly in the form of laws that can limit the processes of power, trust or understanding. Cliques of friends, due to comparatively easy options for exiting the group, are based primarily on trust or understanding; power relationships tend to develop more subtly. The legal system only intervenes in certain cases, such as the escalation of violence. In organizations, however, processes of power, trust and understanding are so unique because they are regulated by the organization's formal structure.

An organization's formal structures prevent those processes of coordination that are based on trust among people. The structures of an organization whose members are bound to it as long as they want to be members offers everyone a guarantee that orders and routines will be followed or coordination will take place, even if people don't trust their counterparts personally. A glance at organizations in developing countries—we need only think of water administration in Jordan, telecommunications companies in the Philippines, or municipal development companies in Senegal—shows that it is considered near pathological in an organization when personal trust predominates and formal structures cannot gain the upper hand over these relationships of trust.

The mechanism of reaching agreements and understanding is also contained by an organization's formal structure. Even if the promoters of the motto, "communication, communication, communication" may find it difficult to accept, organizations use their formal structure to reduce the number of processes required to reach understanding. Both hierarchies and department heads can, as a last resort, retreat to a position secured by the formal structure in order to deflect calls for understanding. An organization's formal structure sets down who is responsible to whom for accountability or information—that's the trick. The formal structure can also be used to curtail processes of reaching understanding that have gotten out of hand.

At first glance, organizations are fertile soil for power struggles over resources, information, access or responsibilities. The formal structure of organizations, however, subdues this phenomenon as well. Hierarchies render constant renegotiation of power positions unnecessary. In disputes, the person who occupies a higher position in the hierarchy can make decisions about the conflict by referring to the rights conferred upon him by the formal structure. It is therefore the formal structure of an organization that prevents the unrestrained explosion of power games.

# 5. How Do You Lead Laterally Through Processes of Change? Applying the Concept

The exercise of power and processes for building trust and understanding take place in a broad variety of situations: for example, in interdepartmental projects, through process chains in companies, in collective bodies such as managing boards or works councils, within the matrix structure of organizations, or in the coordination between cooperation partners from different organizations. In all of these situations, the use of power, trust and understanding mechanisms are subject to their own laws.

A particular application for the concept of lateral leading pertains to processes of planned changes in organizations—meaning what people used to call organizational development and what today is loftily referred to as change management. In many companies and institutions, reorganizations cannot be implemented through hierarchy alone. Often the head of a company does not even have the information to be able to adjust organizational structures, and is therefore forced to involve subaltern employees. Often, however, the new organizational structures, championed by consultants and approved by hierarchies, are worn down by staff members in the operational field in everyday organizational life and deteriorate into paper tigers. This is also why employees are involved in the planning of change processes.

This is where the concept of lateral leading is effective, because it recognizes the central function of hierarchies in organizations, yet also partially dispenses with hierarchical control. At the same time, however, this application is especially problematic, not just because the routines of everyday work are affected, but above all because the framework conditions under which people cooperate are changed. Changing departmental boundaries, hierarchical allocations or standard processes also leads to a change in local rationalities. This also means change, even if slow change, for both the structures of thought and the interests of actors: Processes of *understanding* change. Furthermore, changes in formal structure redistribute the trump cards of power. Departments gain or lose access to knowledge resources, to important external actors, or to communications channels inside the organization. The base of operations for future *power* games is created. Moreover, no one has any experience yet with the new circumstances planned for the organization. *Trust* has to be rebuilt in some cases under these conditions. For the affected members of the organization, these reorganizations put a great deal on the line.

It would be naive to approach planning new organizational structures purely and simply with the categories of understanding, power and trust. When planning new organizational structures—meaning making decisions about the premises of future decisions—very different questions play a role. One issue (and one could say: the main issue) is how communication channels, programs and staff are supposed to interact in the future; which tasks will be taken care of exclusively within the organization and which in cooperation with other organizations; and what new forms of cooperation are supposed to arise between those involved. The categories of power, trust and understanding can, however, provide us with insight into a few aspects of change processes.

|  | **Classical approach to change management** | **Lateral leading approach to change management** |
| --- | --- | --- |
| **Phase: Analysis of the current situation** | Identification of "resisters" and development of strategies to deal with them | Forego concept of "resistance" against change. Routine logic, just like innovation logic, is merely a local rationality within the organization |
| **Phase: Designing interactions** | Discursive exposure of existing power, understanding and trust relations | Acceptance of potential of power, understanding and trust relations |
| **Phase: Implementing solutions** | Only open to possibilities in the phase of problem-solving and solution development. Then foreclose contingency and implement approved solutions | Allow contingency until thought through to the end |

**Table:** An admittedly caricature-like juxtaposition of different approaches in organizational development

## 5.1 The Initial Situation: The Logic of Innovation and Routines in Organizations

The local rationalities that arise from the "old" organizational structures play an important role in the analysis of processes of power, trust and understanding in the course of changing organizational structures. The various constructions of thoughts that make reaching agreement and understanding difficult or easy issue from existing organizational structures. Trust (or distrust) have developed on the basis of the status quo. Trump cards for power are often the result of competence allocations within the organization. This analysis, oriented towards the status quo, is supplemented, expanded and even somewhat overlaid by different logics in change processes.

The promoters of change processes in organizations often work with a relatively simple scheme for differentiation: On one side there are the "innovators" who want to lead a company, administration or hospital to try something completely new, meaning people who are open to change. On the other side there are the "resisters," who stand for the status quo and want to use it to bring the necessary change to the organization. These people are often accused of having an inculcated, if not inborn, tendency to cling to known routines.

If change processes are to be created with lateral leading, it is now necessary to use the same care with which local rationalities of different functional areas are reconstructed to also analyze the local rationalities of various interest groups in change processes. It is only on the basis of the reconstruction of these local rationalities that we can understand routines of trust, processes of understanding, and power games. It quickly becomes apparent that the pressure to move forward with the planned change is not some naturally given necessity for the organization, but rather that the positive attitude towards change comes from the position of the driver in the organization.

The logic of innovation is often driven forward by specific fields within organizations—from the top management, from the staff offices for strategy and organization, and of course from the consultants who are called in to conduct the changes and ensure their successful implementation. These people are "symbols of change" in the organization—the "lasting indication that things can be done differently" (Baecker 1999, 256). This logic of innovation is dominated by ideas about changing existing routines, large comprehensive concepts, and their conflict-free, standardized implementation. This logic of innovation is further exacerbated by ideas about "professional work" that are characteristic for "innovators," by monetary bonuses for "successfully concluded change processes," and by rewards in the form of career promotions.

On the other side there is the logic of routines, which are frequently followed by organizational members on the operational side. They feel very strongly about stabilizing everyday work routines, for example in materials management, production monitoring, manufacturing and installation, or sales. Their ideas about professionalism, bonuses and career opportunities are—despite all management rhetoric to the contrary—largely associated with the successful preservation of these routines. They therefore represent a logic of incremental improvement, security of processes, and attention to the specifics of each department.

There is no reason to view the logic of innovators as somehow superior to that of those who support routines. Discriminating against representatives of routine as "resisters" or "low performers" may play an important role in providing stabilization for a group of innovators, yet it gets in the way of an opportunity to understand, with precision, the local rationalities in a change process and thereby deliver starting points for shifting processes of power, trust and understanding.

The representatives of a rationality of innovation meet those of a rationality of routine on the terrain of change projects, resulting in a "transmission game" with different logics (Ortmann 1994, 64). It is this often contentious "transmission game" that enables innovations to cease being a fantasy of top managers, staff members or consultants; instead, innovation finds expression—even if in a changed form—in the everyday practices of the organization.

## 5.2 The Discussion Phase: The Potential of Lateral Cooperative Relationships

In change management literature, there are often calls for an "unflinching analysis" and "discursive exposure" of the current situation in an organization. It is only on the basis of a precise uncovering of processes of power, trust and understanding, we are told, that it becomes possible to make targeted efforts at change.

What is often overlooked however is that these processes are frequently latent. By latency, we do not mean to follow Freudian psychology and define latency as the unconscious element of a process. It may very well be that the cooperation partners involved are not aware of processes of power, trust and understanding, yet what is far more important is that these processes, even when consciously perceived, cannot (at least not without further effort) be communicated. Communication latency often plays a decisive role, especially for aspects of power, trust and understanding.

An important difference between an organization's formal structure and the informal processes of power, trust and understanding that are often active in lateral leading situations lies in the possibility, or impossibility, of referring to this difference in discussions. Aspects of the formal structure—the official communication channels, the approved programs and the staffing decisions that are announced—can usually be discussed without a problem. People can refer to their hierarchical status to implement a decision, or refer to the strategic imperatives or if-then rules of their organization. Many processes of power, trust and understanding however tend to run on the informal side of the organization, cannot invoke formal assurances, and therefore often cannot be openly and readily discussed.

Communication latency functions as "structural protection" for the processes of power, trust and understanding that tend to take place at the informal level (Luhmann 1995, 336f.). The development of trust between people tends to be impeded rather than helped if this trust is openly expressed ("I trust you") or openly claimed ("Trust me"). Power games change if they are often addressed, and sources of power that are not secured by the formal structure can lose their effectiveness if they are uncovered and laid bare for all to see. The informal processes of understanding in organizations are also only possible in many cases because nobody else knows about them, at least not officially.

How can we deal with the latent potential of many processes of trust, power and understanding?

Existing power, trust and understanding processes between different cooperation partners can typically be tapped into by at least one of the cooperation partners by means of a discussion. Of course, within a department (or perhaps also in a discussion between consultant and a department head, for example), a discussion with other cooperation partners about existing processes of trust, power and understanding is often not all too easy; however, the same barriers to communication do not come up in this situation as they do in the presence of an external cooperation partner, who often comes with other interests.

Existing processes of power, trust and understanding can also be discussed between cooperation partners, but only within a very limited framework. Communication latency (with its structural protection function) does not mean that the participants are not aware of the processes taking place, merely that a discussion about these processes violates official expectations. The violation of this latency then leads for example to consequences, such as the dismissal of talk about a special relationship of trust with an annoyed facial expression, or the denial of the existence of a power source that is not covered by the formal structure. Designers of change processes will therefore think long and hard about whether or not they want to uncover existing latent processes of trust, power and understanding.

Consultants often cannot get a solid insight into existing processes of power, trust and understanding until they can switch back and forth between discussions with people with largely homogeneous opinions (such as representatives from just one department) and people with very heterogeneous views (such as representatives from different departments or organizations). In the latter situation, addressing the latent processes of power, trust and understanding is certainly a risky intervention that is often met with negation, rejection and aggression.

## 5.3 The Creation of Change Processes: The Benefits of Contingency

In the classic, instrumental-rational model of organizations, which dominated organizational development for a long time, the system of change processes is relatively clear. Under this model, a clear definition of the organization's purpose and a precise determination of environmental conditions can lead to a definition of the aim of a change process: the "best solution" for the organization. The inclusion of as many affected people as possible enables this goal to be broken down into manageable targets for each of the sub-units. Change projects, it is assumed, have to be subdivided into discrete project phases such as problem diagnosis, conception, specification and implementation. A phase is typically understood as a self-contained segment of work that ends with a verifiable milestone.

This idealistic approach often does not hold up in organizational practice. Just reaching consensus on what the "best solution" actually is can be quite complicated. The "best solution" varies typically according to the perspective within the organization from which people examine the ostensible problem. No one—not even the hierarchy—can "neutrally" assess which solution is better than all the others. Even if a joint solution is officially announced, it will often be pulverized in the implementation phase, falling victim to existing power relations.

In view of such circumstances, we recommend an approach based on holding "contingency" open for a comparatively long time. Contingency refers to the idea that an event is not inevitable as it is; the event would also be possible in other forms. An analysis of problem A does not unavoidably lead to solution X; it could also lead to solution Y or Z.

Many people commit the error of making early decisions that later stand in the way of cooperation. Early decisions may give rise to concepts to which everyone involved can pay lip service, but such concepts then turn out rather quickly to be a planning mess.

We can keep contingency in change processes visible so that solutions are introduced merely as trial solutions. During the trial, multiple incomplete, even contradictory, concepts can be kicked off at the same time. After all, it is one of the strengths of organizations that they can tolerate even contradictory approaches (see the extensive discussion in Kühl 2018c, forthcoming).

The advantage of trial runs is that new processes of understanding, trust and power can develop in a space that is protected under the aegis of provisionality. Staff in a reorganized field, who are often thrown together, can gain experience with one another in the context of changed communication paths and programs, and develop mutual trust (or distrust). Frequently, other rationalities emerge through these new positions, even if they are only adopted on a provisional basis, leading to new opportunities for understanding. Because power sources are redistributed in a field of cooperation flagged as a trial run, power processes between cooperation partners can also assume another form.

During the course of trying out various solutions, one person or another may crash and burn if they do not turn out to be manageable. A solution can, however, gain quality through the trial process, if the implementation holds the promise of success. Sometimes new strategic directions arise during the trial that have not yet been considered. Appropriate solutions are distilled from the experience.

# 6.
# Outlook—Additional "Search Fields" for Further Developing the Concept of Lateral Leading

The basic characteristics of the lateral leading concept are developed. It will become clear why the concept rests on power, trust and understanding as central mechanisms of influence; at the same time, the list is open for expansions. Unlike other leadership concepts, it is obvious that the idea does not focus merely on minor tactics in an organization's informal side; instead, the connection to the formal structure is systematically developed.

Which lines of development for lateral leading stand out? What specifications will have to be made in the future? The following introduces a few aspects that have to be developed a bit more.

Often organizations are left free to decide how far they want to go with the lateral design of cooperative relationships. When setting up production or installation teams, management decisions often dictate whether these teams will consist of equal team members or whether the team will have a formal supervisor. When establishing project teams, it is possible to set up a hierarchical or lateral structure by granting the project director the according authorization to issue directions. When assembling a mixed management team, for example in development assistance contexts, there are various options available, such as whether decision-making authority is given to the foreign experts instead of the native employees, or whether native and foreign managers should be set at the same hierarchical level in a "twinning" setup.

The management literature is currently promoting the establishment of "lateral leading structures" as a recipe for success under the term "shared leadership" (see for example Pearce/Sims 2002; Ensley et al. 2003; Carson et al. 2007). The general tone seems to be, especially in teams, that the degree of formal equality—meaning "laterality" in organizational structures—correlates positively with effectiveness. It appears that we are witnessing a renaissance of old approaches that are critical of hierarchy, all under a new name.

We believe there is no justification for a general indiscriminate promotion of lateral cooperative relationships. Instead, it seems far more important to make a decision for lateral or hierarchical cooperative relationships based on the organizational situation. What effects on processes of power, trust and understanding stand out? How are lines of conflict changed by a decision for lateral or hierarchical cooperative relationships?

The concept of lateral leading has been tried out and described in very different situations, for example, in process chains in a major international telecommunications company, during the introduction of SAP in a food chemistry company, in the implementation of complex building projects by a real estate fund, in the coordination between product managers and content developers at a global Internet company, in coordination between the works councils in a large international company, or in coordination at the top of a major political party.

Analysis made it clear that although, in all of these processes, the directive-issuing authority of hierarchy did not suffice to set processes in motion, or even to make decisions, hierarchy still continued to serve as a reference point. Even if lateral cooperation partners are hesitant to call upon hierarchy, the operation of power games, the development of relationships of trust, and processes of understanding are shaped by the possibility that the hierarchy could be brought to bear.

This throws up a series of questions, both for application-oriented scholarship as well as practitioners, that relate to the integration of hierarchy when using the mechanisms of power, trust and understanding. How is hierarchy referred to in lateral leading processes within an organization? Which analytical and intervention instruments used by lateral leading are suitable for top-down management? What changes if this approach is implemented from the bottom to the top?

Lateral leading is often used whenever cooperation partners from different companies have to work together. Take as an example automobile companies that try to convince their systems suppliers to invest in the development of new products; the coordination of networks between university institutes and small production companies in nanotechnology; or the management several growth companies by a venture capitalist.

The framework conditions for the lateral leading process with participants from various organizations differ fundamentally from lateral leading processes inside an organization. Within a company, an administration, a hospital or a non-profit organization, the hierarchy always shines through, at least from a distance. This is not the case for lateral relationships between organizations; the framework conditions for lateral leading are influenced much more strongly here than the contracts between the companies, without all aspects of coordination being subject to contractual regulations.

Accordingly, we have to work with a different set of questions for lateral leading processes between organizations: What are a cooperation partner's exit options in a relationship? Would conflicts with other cooperation partners in the same role remain the same or become different? How high is the potential for escalation among the various conflict partners?

# Bibliography

Baecker, Dirk. 1999. *Organisation als System.* Frankfurt a.M.: Suhrkamp.
Blau, Peter M., and W. R. Scott. 1962. *Formal Organizations.* San Francisco: Chandler.
Borges, Jorge L. 1999. "The Analytical Language of John Wilkins." In *Selected Non-Fictions*, edited by Jorge L. Borges, 229–32. New York: Penguin.
Burns, Tom, and George M. Stalker. 1961. *The Management of Innovation.* London: Tavistock.
Carson, Jab Y., Paul E. Tesluk, and Jennifer A. Marrone. 2007. "Shared Leadership in Teams: An Investigation of Antecedent Conditions and Performance." *Academy of Management Journal* 50:1217–34.
Crozier, Michel, and Erhard Friedberg. 1980. *Actors and Systems: The Politics of Collective Action.* Chicago: University of Chicago Press.
Ensley, Michael D., Allison Pearson, and Craig L. Pearce. 2003. "Top Management Team Process, Shared Leadership, and New Venture Performance: A Theoretical Model and Research Agenda." *Human Resource Management Review* 13:329–46.
Fisher, Roger, and Alan Sharpe. 1998. *Getting It Done: How to Lead When You're Not in Charge.* New York: Harper Business Press.
Friedberg, Erhard. 1993. *Le pouvoir et la règle.* Paris: Seuil.

Handy, Charles. 1989. *The Age of Unreason*. Boston: Harvard Business School Press.

Janowitz, Morris. 1959. "Changing Patterns of Organizational Authority: The Military Establishment." *Administrative Science Quarterly* 3:473–93.

Kieser, Alfred, and Lars Leiner. 2009. *On the Impossibility of Collaborative Research—and on the Usefulness of Researchers and Practioners Irritating Each Other*. Mannheim: unpublished manuscript.

Kühl, Stefan. 2013. *Organizations: A Systems Approach*. Farnham: Gower.

Kühl, Stefan. 2017. *When the Monkeys Run the Zoo: The Pitfalls of Flat Hierarchies*. Princeton, Hamburg, Shanghai, Singapore, Versailles, Zurich: Organizational Dialogue Press.

Kühl, Stefan. 2018a (forthcoming). *Sisyphus in Management: The Futile Search for the Optimal Organizational Structure*. Princeton, Hamburg, Shanghai, Singapore, Versailles, Zurich: Organizational Dialogue Press.

Kühl, Stefan. 2018b (forthcoming). *The Rainmaker Effect: Contradictions of the Learning Organization*. Princeton, Hamburg, Shanghai, Singapore, Versailles, Zurich: Organizational Dialogue Press.

Kühl, Stefan. 2018c. *Managing Projects: A Very Brief Introduction*. Princeton, Hamburg, Shanghai, Singapore, Versailles, Zurich: Organizational Dialogue Press.

Lawrence, Paul R., and Jay W. Lorsch. 1967. *Organization and Environment: Managing Differentiation and Integration*. Homewood: Irwin.

Luhmann, Niklas. 1964. *Funktionen und Folgen formaler Organisation*. Berlin: Duncker & Humblot.

Luhmann, Niklas. 1979. *Trust and Power: Two Works.* Chichester, New York: Wiley.

Luhmann, Niklas. 1995. *Social Systems.* Stanford: Stanford University Press.

Luhmann, Niklas. 2002. *Das Erziehungssystem der Gesellschaft.* Frankfurt a.M.: Suhrkamp.

March, James G. 2015. "The First 50 Years and the Next 50 Years of a Behavioral Theory of the Firm: An Interview with James G. March." *Journal of Management Inquiry* 24:149–55.

Mayer, Roger C., James H. Davis, and Schoorman, F. David. 1995. "An Integrative Model of Organizational Trust." *The Academy of Management Review* 20:709–34.

Mechanic, David. 1962. "Sources of Power of Lower Participants in Complex Organizations." *Administrative Science Quarterly* 7:349–64.

Ortmann, Günther. 1994. *Formen der Produktion: Organisation und Rekursivität.* Opladen: WDV.

Pearce, Craig L., and Henry P. Sims. 2002. "Vertical Versus Shared Leadership as Predictors of the Effectiveness of Change Management Teams: an Examination of Aversive, Directive, Transactional, Transformational, and Empowering Leader Behaviors." *Group Dynamics* 6:172–97.

Rapoport, Anatol, and Albert M. Chammah. 1965. *Prisoner's Dilemma: A Study in Conflict and Cooperation.* Ann Arbor: University of Michigan Press.

Schoorman, F. David, Roger C. Mayer, and James H. Davis. 2007. "An Integrative Model of Organizational Trust: Past, Present, and Future." *The Academy of Management Review* 32:344–54.

Simon, Herbert A. 1976. *Administrative Behavior: A Study of Decision Making Processes in Adminstrative Organizations.* 3rd ed. New York: Free Press.

Simpson, Richard L. 1959. "Vertical and Horizontal Communication in Formal Organizations." *Administrative Science Quarterly* 4:188–96.

Strauss, George. 1962. "Tactics of Lateral Relationship: the Purchasing Agent." *Administrative Science Quarterly* 7:161–86.

Thompson, James D. 1967. *Organizations in Action.* New York: McGraw-Hill.

Walton, Richard E. 1966. "Theory of Conflict in Lateral Organizational Relationships." In *Operational Research and the Social Sciences*, edited by J. R. Lawrence, 409–28. London: Tavistock.

Yukl, Gary A., and Cecilia Falbe. 1990. "Influence Tactics and Objectives in Upward, Downward, and Lateral Influence Attempts." *Journal of Applied Psychology* 75:132–40.

www.ingramcontent.com/pod-product-compliance
Lightning Source LLC
Chambersburg PA
CBHW020303030426
42336CB00010B/885